Fun on the Farm

AT THE CROP FARM

By George Pendergast

Gareth Stevens Publishing

Please visit our website, www.garethstevens.com. For a free color catalog of all our high-quality books, call toll free 1-800-542-2595 or fax 1-877-542-2596.

Cataloging-in-Publication Data

Names: Pendergast, George.
Title: At the crop farm / George Pendergast.
Description: New York : Gareth Stevens Publishing, 2017. | Series: Fun on the farm | Includes index.
Identifiers: ISBN 9781482455120 (pbk.) | ISBN 9781482455144 (library bound) | ISBN 9781482455137 (6 pack)
Subjects: LCSH: Crops–Juvenile literature. | Agriculture–Juvenile literature. | Farm life–Juvenile literature.
Classification: LCC SB102.P46 2017 | DDC 630–dc23

First Edition

Published in 2017 by
Gareth Stevens Publishing
111 East 14th Street, Suite 349
New York, NY 10003

Editor: Ryan Nagelhout
Designer: Laura Bowen

Photo credits: Cover, p. 1 Fotokostic/Shutterstock.com; p. 5 Visionsi/Shutterstock.com; p. 7 Dan Thornberg/Shutterstock.com; p. 9 Federico Rostagno/Shutterstock.com; p. 11 TTstudio/Shutterstock.com; p. 13 Fotokostic/Shutterstock.com; pp. 15, 24 Billion Photos; p. 17 stoonn/Shutterstock.com; pp. 19, 24 Ruud Morijn/Shutterstock.com; pp. 21, 24 zhuda/Shutterstock.com; p. 23 monofaction/Shutterstock.com.

Printed in the United States of America

CPSIA compliance information: Batch #CW17GS: For further information contact Gareth Stevens, New York, New York at 1-800-542-2595.

Contents

Farmers grow
plants we eat.
These are called crops.

Most grow in summer.

They need water to grow.

They also need light.
This comes
from the sun.

Crops grow
in big open spaces.
These are called fields.

Farmers put seeds
in the ground.
This is planting.

Many farmers
plant corn.
It is often yellow.

Beans grow on vines.

Rice is very small.
It grows in lots of water.

Some crops grow
without dirt, too!

Words to Know

beans

rice

seeds

Index